MW00953675

CONTENTS

ALEXANDER-GRACE EDUCATION

ALEXANDER-GRACE EDUCATION

Understanding the MAP Tests

The NWEA MAP (Measures of Academic Progress) test is an adaptive assessment that is designed to measure student growth and progress in a variety of subject areas. The test is taken by millions of students across the United States and is widely used by educators to help inform instruction and measure student outcomes. The NWEA MAP test is administered online and provides immediate feedback on student performance, allowing teachers to adjust their teaching strategies and provide targeted support to individual students.

The NWEA MAP test is unique in that it is adaptive, which means that the difficulty of the questions adjusts based on the student's responses. This allows the test to be more personalized to each student's abilities and provides a more accurate measure of their knowledge and skills. The test covers a range of subject areas, including mathematics, reading, language usage, and science, and is administered multiple times throughout the school year. This allows teachers to track student progress and growth over time and make data-driven decisions to improve student outcomes.

Purpose and Benefits of MAP Testing

The primary purpose of the MAP Test is to provide valuable insights into a student's learning and academic progress. By offering a detailed analysis of a student's performance in reading, language usage, mathematics, and science, the test helps teachers tailor their instruction to meet individual needs. The MAP Test also serves as a benchmarking tool, allowing schools and districts to compare their students' performance with national norms and other local institutions.

This data-driven approach enables educators to make informed decisions about curriculum, instructional methods, and resource allocation, ultimately leading to improved student outcomes. Additionally, the MAP Test can help identify gifted students who may benefit from advanced or accelerated programs, as well as students who may require additional support or interventions.

Test Format and Content

The MAP Test is divided into four primary content areas: reading, language usage, mathematics, and science. Each section consists of multiple-choice questions that cover various topics and skills within the respective subject. The test is untimed, allowing students to work at their own pace and ensuring a lower level of test anxiety. The computer-adaptive nature of the MAP Test ensures that the difficulty of questions adjusts based on a student's performance, making it suitable for students of all ability levels. As a result, the MAP Test not only evaluates a student's mastery of grade-level content but also assesses their readiness for more advanced material.

Adaptive Testing and Scoring System

One of the unique aspects of the MAP Test is its adaptive testing system. As students answer questions, the test adjusts the difficulty of subsequent questions based on their performance. This adaptive nature allows the test to home in on a student's true ability level, providing more accurate and meaningful results. The MAP Test uses a RIT (Rasch Unit) scale to measure student achievement, which is an equal-interval scale that allows for easy comparison of scores across grade levels and subjects. This scoring system allows educators and parents to track a student's growth over time, making it an invaluable tool for understanding academic progress and setting individualized learning goals.

Preparing for Success on the MAP Test

Effective preparation for the MAP Test involves a combination of understanding the test format, mastering content knowledge, and developing test-taking strategies. This test prep book is designed to provide students with comprehensive guidance on each content area, offering targeted instruction and practice questions to build confidence and ensure success. Additionally, the book includes test-taking tips and strategies to help students approach the test with a calm and focused mindset. By working through this book and dedicating time to consistent practice, students will be well-equipped to excel on the MAP Test and achieve their academic goals.

Note that, since there is no cap to the level that a student can work to in preparation for this test, there is no 'completion' of content, as students can simply do questions from grades above in preparation. It should be noted that students are not expected to work far above grade level to succeed in this test, as consistent correct answers are more relevant.

What Is Contained Within this Book?

Within this book you will find 320 questions based off content which would be found within the MAP test your student will take. The content found in this book will be the equivalent of grade 7 level. Note that since this test is adaptive, some students may benefit by looking at several grade levels of content, not just their own.

At the end of the book will contain answers alongside explanations. It is recommended to look and check your answers thoroughly in regular intervals to make sure you improve as similar questions come up.

Topic 1 - Figurative Language

1.1) What type of figurative language is used in the sentence: 'The classroom was a zoo'?

☐ Idiom

☐ Metaphor

☐ Simile

☐ Hyperbole

1.2) Identify the figurative language: 'He was as brave as a lion'?

☐ Metaphor

☐ Symbolism

☐ Simile

☐ Hyperbole

1.3) What does the idiom 'break the ice' mean?

☐ End a relationship

☐ Break something

☐ Cool down

☐ Start a conversation

1.4) What type of figurative language is used in the sentence: 'She is drowning in a sea of grief'?

☐ Simile

☐ Metaphor

☐ Symbolism

☐ Hyperbole

1.5) Identify the figurative language: 'It's raining cats and dogs'?

☐ Metaphor

☐ Hyperbole

☐ Idiom

☐ Simile

1.6) What does the hyperbole 'I have a ton of homework' mean?

☐ I have a small amount of homework

☐ I have no homework

☐ I have a manageable amount of homework

☐ I have a lot of homework

1.7) What type of figurative language is used in the sentence: 'The wind whispered through the trees'?

☐ Metaphor

☐ Hyperbole

☐ Simile

☐ Personification

1.8) Identify the figurative language: 'Her smile was as bright as the sun'?

☐ Metaphor

☐ Symbolism

☐ Simile

☐ Idiom

1.9) What does the symbolism of a dove typically represent?

☐ Strength

☐ Sadness

☐ Peace

☐ Anger

1.10) What type of figurative language is used in the sentence: 'He has a heart of stone'?

☐ Simile

☐ Metaphor

☐ Personification

☐ Hyperbole

1.11) What type of figurative language is used in the sentence: 'The world is my oyster'?

☐ Metaphor

☐ Idiom

☐ Simile

☐ Hyperbole

1.12) Identify the figurative language: 'He ran faster than a speeding bullet'?

☐ Hyperbole

☐ Metaphor

☐ Simile

☐ Symbolism

1.13) What does the idiom 'hit the nail on the head' mean?

☐ Miss the point

☐ Get something exactly right

☐ Get confused

☐ Hit something hard

1.14) What type of figurative language is used in the sentence: 'The stars danced in the sky'?

☐ Metaphor

☐ Hyperbole

☐ Simile

☐ Personification

1.15) Identify the figurative language: 'She was a rock during the crisis'?

☐ Hyperbole

☐ Simile

☐ Idiom

☐ Metaphor

1.16) What does the hyperbole 'I'm so hungry I could eat a horse' mean?

☐ I'm not hungry

☐ I'm very hungry

☐ I don't like food

☐ I want a small meal

1.17) What type of figurative language is used in the sentence: 'The leaves waved in the wind'?

☐ Hyperbole

☐ Metaphor

☐ Personification

☐ Simile

1.18) Identify the figurative language: 'He is as strong as an ox'?

☐ Metaphor

☐ Simile

☐ Symbolism

☐ Idiom

1.19) What does the symbolism of a red rose typically represent?

☐ Fear

☐ Love

☐ Hate

☐ Sadness

1.20) What type of figurative language is used in the sentence: 'Her voice is music to my ears'?

☐ Hyperbole

☐ Personification

☐ Metaphor

☐ Simile

1.21) What type of figurative language is used in the sentence: 'The fire ran wild'?

☐ Simile

☐ Hyperbole

☐ Personification

☐ Metaphor

1.22) Identify the figurative language: 'She is as light as a feather'?

☐ Idiom

☐ Simile

☐ Metaphor

☐ Symbolism

1.23) What does the idiom 'spill the beans' mean?

☐ Reveal a secret

☐ Hide something

☐ Cook dinner

☐ Make a mess

1.24) What type of figurative language is used in the sentence: 'The clock yelled at me to wake up'?

☐ Hyperbole

☐ Personification

☐ Metaphor

☐ Simile

1.25) Identify the figurative language: 'His words were a dagger to my heart'?

☐ Hyperbole

☐ Metaphor

☐ Simile

☐ Idiom

1.26) What does the hyperbole 'I've told you a million times' mean?

☐ I've told you once

☐ I've never told you

☐ I've told you many times

☐ I've told you a few times

1.27) What type of figurative language is used in the sentence: 'The thunder was a drum in the night'?

☐ Metaphor

☐ Personification

☐ Simile

☐ Hyperbole

1.28) Identify the figurative language: 'She sings like an angel'?

☐ Idiom

☐ Metaphor

☐ Simile

☐ Symbolism

1.29) What does the symbolism of an olive branch typically represent?

☐ Anger

☐ War

☐ Strength

☐ Peace

1.30) What type of figurative language is used in the sentence: 'His smile was a ray of sunshine'?

☐ Hyperbole

☐ Metaphor

☐ Personification

☐ Simile

1.31) What type of figurative language is used in the sentence: 'The stars in the sky were diamonds'?

☐ Simile

☐ Hyperbole

☐ Personification

☐ Metaphor

1.32) Identify the figurative language: 'He eats like a pig'?

☐ Simile

☐ Idiom

☐ Metaphor

☐ Symbolism

1.33) What does the idiom 'burning the midnight oil' mean?

☐ Setting something on fire

☐ Working late into the night

☐ Cooking dinner

☐ Sleeping early

1.34) What type of figurative language is used in the sentence: 'The flowers nodded their heads in the breeze'?

☐ Simile

☐ Hyperbole

☐ Metaphor

☐ Personification

1.35) Identify the figurative language: 'Time is a thief'?

☐ Simile

☐ Hyperbole

☐ Metaphor

☐ Idiom

1.36) What does the hyperbole 'I could sleep for a year' mean?

☐ I am not tired

☐ I don't need sleep

☐ I am very tired

☐ I slept well

1.37) What type of figurative language is used in the sentence: 'The car's engine roared to life'?

☐ Metaphor

☐ Simile

☐ Personification

☐ Hyperbole

1.38) Identify the figurative language: 'Her eyes were as blue as the ocean'?

☐ Metaphor

☐ Simile

☐ Symbolism

☐ Idiom

1.39) What does the symbolism of a broken chain typically represent?

☐ Freedom

☐ Unity

☐ Bondage

☐ Strength

1.40) What type of figurative language is used in the sentence: 'The snow was a white blanket over the town'?

☐ Simile

☐ Metaphor

☐ Personification

☐ Hyperbole

Topic 1 - Answers

Question Number	Answer	Explanation
1.1	Metaphor	"The classroom was a zoo" is a metaphor.
1.2	Simile	"He was as brave as a lion" is a simile.
1.3	Start a conversation	"Break the ice" means to start a conversation.
1.4	Metaphor	"She is drowning in a sea of grief" is a metaphor.
1.5	Idiom	"It's raining cats and dogs" is an idiom.
1.6	I have a lot of homework	"I have a ton of homework" means I have a lot of homework.
1.7	Personification	"The wind whispered through the trees" is personification.
1.8	Simile	"Her smile was as bright as the sun" is a simile.
1.9	Peace	A dove typically represents peace.
1.10	Metaphor	"He has a heart of stone" is a metaphor.
1.11	Metaphor	"The world is my oyster" is a metaphor.
1.12	Hyperbole	"He ran faster than a speeding bullet" is a hyperbole.
1.13	Get something exactly right	"Hit the nail on the head" means get something exactly right.
1.14	Personification	"The stars danced in the sky" is personification.
1.15	Metaphor	"She was a rock during the crisis" is a metaphor.
1.16	I'm very hungry	"I'm so hungry I could eat a horse" means I'm very hungry.
1.17	Personification	"The leaves waved in the wind" is personification.
1.18	Simile	"He is as strong as an ox" is a simile.

1.19	Love	A red rose typically represents love.
1.20	Metaphor	"Her voice is music to my ears" is a metaphor.
1.21	Personification	"The fire ran wild" is personification.
1.22	Simile	"She is as light as a feather" is a simile.
1.23	Reveal a secret	"Spill the beans" means reveal a secret.
1.24	Personification	"The clock yelled at me to wake up" is personification.
1.25	Metaphor	"His words were a dagger to my heart" is a metaphor.
1.26	I've told you many times	"I've told you a million times" means I've told you many times.
1.27	Metaphor	"The thunder was a drum in the night" is a metaphor.
1.28	Simile	"She sings like an angel" is a simile.
1.29	Peace	An olive branch typically represents peace.
1.30	Metaphor	"His smile was a ray of sunshine" is a metaphor.
1.31	Metaphor	"The stars in the sky were diamonds" is a metaphor.
1.32	Simile	"He eats like a pig" is a simile.
1.33	Working late into the night	"Burning the midnight oil" means working late into the night.
1.34	Personification	"The flowers nodded their heads in the breeze" is personification.
1.35	Metaphor	"Time is a thief" is a metaphor.
1.36	I am very tired	"I could sleep for a year" means I am very tired.
1.37	Personification	"The car's engine roared to life" is personification.
1.38	Simile	"Her eyes were as blue as the ocean" is a simile.
1.39	Freedom	A broken chain typically represents freedom.
1.40	Metaphor	"The snow was a white blanket over the town" is a metaphor.

ALEXANDER-GRACE EDUCATION

Topic 2 – Sentence Structure and Types

2.1) What type of sentence is this: 'The dog barked loudly.'?

☐ Complex

☐ Simple

☐ Compound

☐ Compound-Complex

2.2) Identify the sentence type: 'She went to the store, and he stayed home.'?

☐ Simple

☐ Compound-Complex

☐ Compound

☐ Complex

2.3) What type of sentence is this: 'Although it was raining, they went for a walk.'?

☐ Compound

☐ Complex

☐ Simple

☐ Compound-Complex

2.4) Identify the sentence type: 'I like coffee, but she likes tea.'?

☐ Simple

☐ Compound-Complex

☐ Compound

☐ Complex

2.5) What type of sentence is this: 'When the bell rang, the students left the classroom, and the teacher sighed.'?

☐ Compound

☐ Complex

☐ Compound-Complex

☐ Simple

2.6) Identify the sentence type: 'Please close the door.'?

☐ Interrogative

☐ Exclamatory

☐ Imperative

☐ Declarative

2.7) What type of sentence is this: 'Do you want to play a game?'?

☐ Imperative

☐ Exclamatory

☐ Declarative

☐ Interrogative

2.8) Identify the sentence type: 'Wow, that was amazing!'?

□ Imperative

□ Exclamatory

□ Interrogative

□ Declarative

2.9) What type of sentence is this: 'The sun is shining brightly.'?

□ Interrogative

□ Imperative

□ Exclamatory

□ Declarative

2.10) Identify the sentence type: 'She cleaned the house and he cooked dinner.'?

□ Complex

□ Compound-Complex

□ Compound

□ Simple

2.11) What type of sentence is this: 'After the game ended, we went out for ice cream.'?

□ Complex

□ Simple

□ Compound-Complex

□ Compound

2.12) Identify the sentence type: 'She reads books, and he watches movies.'?

☐ Complex

☐ Simple

☐ Compound-Complex

☐ Compound

2.13) What type of sentence is this: 'Close the window, please.'?

☐ Exclamatory

☐ Imperative

☐ Interrogative

☐ Declarative

2.14) Identify the sentence type: 'Why did you do that?'?

☐ Declarative

☐ Interrogative

☐ Imperative

☐ Exclamatory

2.15) What type of sentence is this: 'He didn't like the movie, but he enjoyed the popcorn.'?

☐ Compound-Complex

☐ Complex

☐ Simple

☐ Compound

2.16) Identify the sentence type: 'If you study hard, you will pass the exam.'?

☐ Complex

☐ Compound-Complex

☐ Simple

☐ Compound

2.17) What type of sentence is this: 'I can't believe we won the game!'?

☐ Exclamatory

☐ Interrogative

☐ Imperative

☐ Declarative

2.18) Identify the sentence type: 'The cat sat on the mat.'?

☐ Compound

☐ Compound-Complex

☐ Complex

☐ Simple

2.19) What type of sentence is this: 'Can you help me with my homework?'?

☐ Imperative

☐ Interrogative

☐ Exclamatory

☐ Declarative

2.20) Identify the sentence type: 'She was tired, so she went to bed early.'?

☐ Complex

☐ Compound-Complex

☐ Simple

☐ Compound

2.21) What type of sentence is this: 'Although it was late, she continued to study, and he went to bed.'?

☐ Complex

☐ Compound-Complex

☐ Compound

☐ Simple

2.22) Identify the sentence type: 'Run as fast as you can!'?

☐ Imperative

☐ Declarative

☐ Exclamatory

☐ Interrogative

2.23) What type of sentence is this: 'She smiled and waved at her friend.'?

☐ Compound-Complex

☐ Compound

☐ Simple

☐ Complex

2.24) Identify the sentence type: 'If it rains tomorrow, we will cancel the picnic.'?

☐ Compound-Complex

☐ Compound

☐ Complex

☐ Simple

2.25) What type of sentence is this: 'Wow, that was an incredible performance!'?

☐ Declarative

☐ Exclamatory

☐ Imperative

☐ Interrogative

2.26) Identify the sentence type: 'The children played in the park, and the parents watched.'?

□ Compound

□ Simple

□ Compound-Complex

□ Complex

2.27) What type of sentence is this: 'Where did you find that book?'?

□ Imperative

□ Declarative

□ Exclamatory

□ Interrogative

2.28) Identify the sentence type: 'The train arrived on time, but the bus was late.'?

□ Complex

□ Compound-Complex

□ Compound

□ Simple

2.29) What type of sentence is this: 'Please pass the salt.'?

□ Exclamatory

□ Declarative

□ Imperative

□ Interrogative

2.30) Identify the sentence type: 'The sun was setting, the birds were singing, and the air was cool.'?

☐ Complex

☐ Simple

☐ Compound

☐ Compound-Complex

2.31) What type of sentence is this: 'When I arrived home, the dog barked, and the cat ran away.'?

☐ Compound

☐ Compound-Complex

☐ Simple

☐ Complex

2.32) Identify the sentence type: 'Shut the door!'?

☐ Interrogative

☐ Exclamatory

☐ Imperative

☐ Declarative

2.33) What type of sentence is this: 'She loves to read, and he enjoys playing sports.'?

□ Simple

□ Complex

□ Compound

□ Compound-Complex

2.34) Identify the sentence type: 'Is it going to rain today?'?

□ Imperative

□ Exclamatory

□ Declarative

□ Interrogative

2.35) What type of sentence is this: 'The flowers are blooming, and the birds are singing.'?

□ Compound-Complex

□ Complex

□ Compound

□ Simple

2.36) Identify the sentence type: 'Get out of my room!'?

□ Imperative

□ Interrogative

□ Exclamatory

□ Declarative

2.37) What type of sentence is this: 'The children were playing outside while their parents cooked dinner.'?

☐ Compound

☐ Complex

☐ Compound-Complex

☐ Simple

2.38) Identify the sentence type: 'She studied hard, so she passed the exam.'?

☐ Compound-Complex

☐ Simple

☐ Complex

☐ Compound

2.39) What type of sentence is this: 'If you see my keys, let me know.'?

☐ Complex

☐ Simple

☐ Compound-Complex

☐ Compound

2.40) Identify the sentence type: 'The sky is clear, the stars are bright, and the air is cool.'?

☐ Simple

☐ Compound

☐ Compound-Complex

☐ Complex

Topic 2 - Answers

Question Number	Answer	Explanation
2.1	Simple	"The dog barked loudly." is a simple sentence.
2.2	Compound	"She went to the store, and he stayed home." is a compound sentence.
2.3	Complex	"Although it was raining, they went for a walk." is a complex sentence.
2.4	Compound	"I like coffee, but she likes tea." is a compound sentence.
2.5	Compound-Complex	"When the bell rang, the students left the classroom, and the teacher sighed." is a compound-complex sentence.
2.6	Imperative	"Please close the door." is an imperative sentence.
2.7	Interrogative	"Do you want to play a game?" is an interrogative sentence.
2.8	Exclamatory	"Wow, that was amazing!" is an exclamatory sentence.
2.9	Declarative	"The sun is shining brightly." is a declarative sentence.
2.10	Compound	"She cleaned the house and he cooked dinner." is a compound sentence.
2.11	Complex	"After the game ended, we went out for ice cream." is a complex sentence.
2.12	Compound	"She reads books, and he watches movies." is a compound sentence.
2.13	Imperative	"Close the window, please." is an imperative sentence.
2.14	Interrogative	"Why did you do that?" is an interrogative sentence.
2.15	Compound	"He didn't like the movie, but he enjoyed the popcorn." is a compound sentence.
2.16	Complex	"If you study hard, you will pass the exam." is a complex sentence.
2.17	Exclamatory	"I can't believe we won the game!" is an exclamatory sentence.
2.18	Simple	"The cat sat on the mat." is a simple sentence.

2.19	Interrogative	"Can you help me with my homework?" is an interrogative sentence.
2.20	Compound	"She was tired, so she went to bed early." is a compound sentence.
2.21	Compound-Complex	"Although it was late, she continued to study, and he went to bed." is a compound-complex sentence.
2.22	Exclamatory	"Run as fast as you can!" is an exclamatory sentence.
2.23	Simple	"She smiled and waved at her friend." is a simple sentence.
2.24	Complex	"If it rains tomorrow, we will cancel the picnic." is a complex sentence.
2.25	Exclamatory	"Wow, that was an incredible performance!" is an exclamatory sentence.
2.26	Compound	"The children played in the park, and the parents watched." is a compound sentence.
2.27	Interrogative	"Where did you find that book?" is an interrogative sentence.
2.28	Compound	"The train arrived on time, but the bus was late." is a compound sentence.
2.29	Imperative	"Please pass the salt." is an imperative sentence.
2.30	Compound-Complex	"The sun was setting, the birds were singing, and the air was cool." is a compound-complex sentence.
2.31	Compound-Complex	"When I arrived home, the dog barked, and the cat ran away." is a compound-complex sentence.
2.32	Imperative	"Shut the door!" is an imperative sentence.
2.33	Compound	"She loves to read, and he enjoys playing sports." is a compound sentence.
2.34	Interrogative	"Is it going to rain today?" is an interrogative sentence.
2.35	Compound	"The flowers are blooming, and the birds are singing." is a compound sentence.
2.36	Exclamatory	"Get out of my room!" is an exclamatory sentence.
2.37	Complex	"The children were playing outside while their parents cooked dinner." is a complex sentence.
2.38	Compound	"She studied hard, so she passed the exam." is a compound sentence.
2.39	Complex	"If you see my keys, let me know." is a complex sentence.
2.40	Compound-Complex	"The sky is clear, the stars are bright, and the air is cool." is a compound-complex sentence.

Topic 3 – Synonyms and Antonyms

3.1) What is a synonym for 'abundant'?

☐ Few

☐ Limited

☐ Plentiful

☐ Scarce

3.2) What is an antonym for 'benevolent'?

☐ Generous

☐ Cruel

☐ Charitable

☐ Kind

3.3) Choose the synonym for 'candid'.

☐ Deceitful

☐ Sneaky

☐ Dishonest

☐ Honest

3.4) What is an antonym for 'debilitating'?

☐ Damaging

☐ Weakening

☐ Strengthening

☐ Crippling

3.5) What is a synonym for 'eccentric'?

☐ Regular

☐ Unconventional

☐ Common

☐ Normal

3.6) Choose the antonym for 'frivolous'.

☐ Serious

☐ Trivial

☐ Unimportant

☐ Silly

3.7) What is a synonym for 'garrulous'?

☐ Silent

☐ Reserved

☐ Quiet

☐ Talkative

3.8) What is an antonym for 'harmonious'?

☐ Melodious

☐ Discordant

☐ Musical

☐ Agreeable

3.9) Choose the synonym for 'imminent'.

☐ Remote

☐ Far

☐ Distant

☐ Approaching

3.10) What is an antonym for 'juxtapose'?

☐ Place side by side

☐ Separate

☐ Compare

☐ Contrast

3.11) What is a synonym for 'keen'?

☐ Disinterested

☐ Eager

☐ Unenthusiastic

☐ Dull

3.12) What is an antonym for 'lethargic'?

☐ Tired

☐ Sluggish

☐ Energetic

☐ Lazy

3.13) Choose the synonym for 'meticulous'.

□ Careless

□ Negligent

□ Detailed

□ Messy

3.14) What is an antonym for 'notorious'?

□ Famous

□ Unknown

□ Well-known

□ Infamous

3.15) What is a synonym for 'obscure'?

□ Obvious

□ Clear

□ Unclear

□ Apparent

3.16) Choose the antonym for 'paragon'.

□ Example

□ Ideal

□ Flaw

□ Model

3.17) What is a synonym for 'quaint'?

☐ Charming

☐ Modern

☐ Common

☐ Ordinary

3.18) What is an antonym for 'reclusive'?

☐ Sociable

☐ Lonely

☐ Isolated

☐ Alone

3.19) Choose the synonym for 'skeptical'.

☐ Trusting

☐ Doubtful

☐ Certain

☐ Believing

3.20) What is an antonym for 'tangible'?

☐ Physical

☐ Concrete

☐ Abstract

☐ Real

3.21) What is a synonym for 'unanimous'?

☐ Divided

☐ Disagreeing

☐ Uncertain

☐ Agreed

3.22) What is an antonym for 'venerable'?

☐ Adored

☐ Respected

☐ Honored

☐ Disrespected

3.23) Choose the synonym for 'witty'.

☐ Serious

☐ Clever

☐ Unfunny

☐ Dull

3.24) What is an antonym for 'yearn'?

☐ Desire

☐ Long

☐ Crave

☐ Dislike

3.25) What is a synonym for 'zealous'?

☐ Passionate

☐ Unenthusiastic

☐ Apathetic

☐ Indifferent

3.26) Choose the antonym for 'adversity'.

☐ Difficulty

☐ Hardship

☐ Prosperity

☐ Misfortune

3.27) What is a synonym for 'brusque'?

☐ Polite

☐ Gracious

☐ Blunt

☐ Courteous

3.28) What is an antonym for 'conspicuous'?

☐ Hidden

☐ Visible

☐ Noticeable

☐ Prominent

3.29) Choose the synonym for 'diligent'.

☐ Hardworking

☐ Negligent

☐ Idle

☐ Lazy

3.30) What is an antonym for 'exemplary'?

☐ Model

☐ Deplorable

☐ Ideal

☐ Admirable

3.31) What is a synonym for 'frugal'?

☐ Lavish

☐ Thrifty

☐ Wasteful

☐ Extravagant

3.32) What is an antonym for 'hostile'?

☐ Friendly

☐ Unfriendly

☐ Antagonistic

☐ Hostile

3.33) Choose the synonym for 'inevitable'.

□ Unlikely

□ Avoidable

□ Likely

□ Unavoidable

3.34) What is an antonym for 'jubilant'?

□ Happy

□ Miserable

□ Triumphant

□ Joyful

3.35) What is a synonym for 'lucid'?

□ Clear

□ Unclear

□ Obscure

□ Confused

3.36) Choose the antonym for 'malicious'.

□ Benevolent

□ Malevolent

□ Spiteful

□ Hateful

3.37) What is a synonym for 'nostalgic'?

☐ Wistful

☐ Unemotional

☐ Unsentimental

☐ Indifferent

3.38) What is an antonym for 'optimistic'?

☐ Pessimistic

☐ Confident

☐ Positive

☐ Hopeful

3.39) Choose the synonym for 'prudent'.

☐ Foolish

☐ Reckless

☐ Wise

☐ Careless

3.40) What is an antonym for 'resilient'?

☐ Fragile

☐ Tough

☐ Strong

☐ Robust

Topic 3 - Answers

Question Number	Answer	Explanation
3.1	Plentiful	A synonym for "abundant" is "plentiful".
3.2	Cruel	An antonym for "benevolent" is "cruel".
3.3	Honest	A synonym for "candid" is "honest".
3.4	Strengthening	An antonym for "debilitating" is "strengthening".
3.5	Unconventional	A synonym for "eccentric" is "unconventional".
3.6	Serious	An antonym for "frivolous" is "serious".
3.7	Talkative	A synonym for "garrulous" is "talkative".
3.8	Discordant	An antonym for "harmonious" is "discordant".
3.9	Approaching	A synonym for "imminent" is "approaching".
3.10	Separate	An antonym for "juxtapose" is "separate".
3.11	Eager	A synonym for "keen" is "eager".
3.12	Energetic	An antonym for "lethargic" is "energetic".
3.13	Detailed	A synonym for "meticulous" is "detailed".
3.14	Unknown	An antonym for "notorious" is "unknown".
3.15	Unclear	A synonym for "obscure" is "unclear".
3.16	Flaw	An antonym for "paragon" is "flaw".
3.17	Charming	A synonym for "quaint" is "charming".
3.18	Sociable	An antonym for "reclusive" is "sociable".

3.19	Doubtful	A synonym for "skeptical" is "doubtful".
3.20	Abstract	An antonym for "tangible" is "abstract".
3.21	Agreed	A synonym for "unanimous" is "agreed".
3.22	Disrespected	An antonym for "venerable" is "disrespected".
3.23	Clever	A synonym for "witty" is "clever".
3.24	Dislike	An antonym for "yearn" is "dislike".
3.25	Passionate	A synonym for "zealous" is "passionate".
3.26	Prosperity	An antonym for "adversity" is "prosperity".
3.27	Blunt	A synonym for "brusque" is "blunt".
3.28	Hidden	An antonym for "conspicuous" is "hidden".
3.29	Hardworking	A synonym for "diligent" is "hardworking".
3.30	Deplorable	An antonym for "exemplary" is "deplorable".
3.31	Thrifty	A synonym for "frugal" is "thrifty".
3.32	Friendly	An antonym for "hostile" is "friendly".
3.33	Unavoidable	A synonym for "inevitable" is "unavoidable".
3.34	Miserable	An antonym for "jubilant" is "miserable".
3.35	Clear	A synonym for "lucid" is "clear".
3.36	Benevolent	An antonym for "malicious" is "benevolent".
3.37	Wistful	A synonym for "nostalgic" is "wistful".
3.38	Pessimistic	An antonym for "optimistic" is "pessimistic".
3.39	Wise	A synonym for "prudent" is "wise".
3.40	Fragile	An antonym for "resilient" is "fragile".

Topic 4 – Punctuation and Grammar

4.1) Which sentence uses commas correctly?

☐ After dinner we went, to the movies.

☐ After, dinner we went to the movies.

☐ After dinner, we went to the movies.

☐ After dinner we went to, the movies.

4.2) Which sentence avoids a comma splice?

☐ I went, to the store and I bought some milk.

☐ I went to the store, and bought some milk.

☐ I went to the store, I bought some milk.

☐ I went to the store, and I bought some milk.

4.3) Where should the semicolon be placed in this sentence: 'I have a big test tomorrow I can't go out tonight'?

☐ test;

☐ go;

☐ tomorrow;

☐ big;

4.4) Which sentence correctly uses a colon?

☐ I need: the following items milk, eggs, and bread.

☐ I need the: following items, milk, eggs, and bread.

☐ I need the following items milk, eggs: and bread.

☐ I need the following items: milk, eggs, and bread.

4.5) Which sentence correctly uses parentheses?

☐ My brother who is a year older than me (is very tall).

☐ My brother (who is a year older than me) is very tall.

☐ My brother (who is a year older than me) is very tall).

☐ My brother (who is a year older) than me is very tall.

4.6) Where should the quotation marks be placed in this sentence: 'She said, I can't believe it's already Friday!'?

☐ She said, 'I can't believe it's already Friday!'

☐ She said, I can't believe 'it's already Friday!'

☐ 'She said, I can't believe it's already Friday!'

☐ She said, I can't believe it's already Friday!'

4.7) Which sentence correctly uses a comma after an introductory phrase?

☐ After the movie we went out, for ice cream.

☐ After the movie, we went out for ice cream.

☐ After, the movie we went out for ice cream.

☐ After the movie we went out for, ice cream.

4.8) Which sentence avoids a fragment?

☐ I went to bed early. Because I was tired.

☐ Because I was tired. I went to bed early.

☐ Because I was tired. Went to bed early.

☐ Because I was tired, I went to bed early.

4.9) Where should the commas be placed in this sentence: 'During the summer we like to swim, fish, and hike'?

☐ During the summer, we like to swim, fish, and hike.

☐ During the summer we, like to swim fish, and hike.

☐ During the summer we like, to swim fish, and hike.

☐ During, the summer we like to swim fish, and hike.

4.10) Which sentence correctly uses a semicolon?

☐ I have a test tomorrow; I can't go out tonight.

☐ I have a test tomorrow, I can't go out tonight.

☐ I have; a test tomorrow I can't go out tonight.

☐ I have a test; tomorrow I can't go out tonight.

4.11) Which sentence uses commas correctly?

☐ Before leaving the kids cleaned, their rooms.

☐ Before leaving, the kids cleaned their rooms.

☐ Before, leaving the kids cleaned their rooms.

☐ Before leaving the kids, cleaned their rooms.

4.12) Which sentence avoids a comma splice?

☐ She loves to, read and she visits the library often.

☐ She loves to read, and she visits the library often.

☐ She loves to read, she visits the library often.

☐ She loves to read and, she visits the library often.

4.13) Where should the semicolon be placed in this sentence: 'I have to clean the house I have guests coming over'?

□ guests;

□ to;

□ house;

□ clean;

4.14) Which sentence correctly uses a colon?

□ Remember to bring your notebook, a pen: and a calculator.

□ Remember to bring: your notebook, a pen, and a calculator.

□ Remember: to bring your notebook, a pen, and a calculator.

□ Remember to bring your: notebook, a pen, and a calculator.

4.15) Which sentence correctly uses parentheses?

□ The author who wrote (the famous series) will be signing books.

□ The author (who wrote the famous series) will be signing books).

□ The author (who wrote the famous series) will be signing books.

□ The author (who wrote the famous series will be) signing books.

4.16) Where should the quotation marks be placed in this sentence: 'He shouted, Watch out!'?

□ 'He shouted, Watch out!'

□ He shouted, Watch out!'

□ He shouted, 'Watch out!'

□ He 'shouted, Watch out!'

4.17) Which sentence correctly uses a comma after an introductory phrase?

□ In the morning we will, start the hike.

□ In the morning, we will start the hike.

□ In, the morning we will start the hike.

□ In the morning we will start, the hike.

4.18) Which sentence avoids a fragment?

□ When I finished my homework. I went to bed.

□ When I finished my homework, I went to bed.

□ When I finished. My homework I went to bed.

□ When I finished my homework. Went to bed.

4.19) Where should the commas be placed in this sentence: 'For dinner we had steak, potatoes and salad'?

□ For dinner we had steak, potatoes and, salad.

□ For dinner, we had steak, potatoes, and salad.

□ For dinner we had, steak potatoes, and salad.

□ For, dinner we had steak potatoes, and salad.

4.20) Which sentence correctly uses a semicolon?

□ We wanted to go to the park; however, it started to rain.

□ We wanted; to go to the park however, it started to rain.

□ We wanted to go; to the park, however it started to rain.

□ We wanted to go to the park, however it started to rain.

4.21) Which sentence uses commas correctly?

□ On, our trip we visited Paris, London, and Rome.

□ On our trip, we visited Paris, London, and Rome.

□ On our trip we visited Paris, London and, Rome.

□ On our trip we visited, Paris, London, and Rome.

4.22) Which sentence avoids a comma splice?

□ She studied hard, she passed the test.

□ She studied, hard so she passed the test.

□ She studied hard, so she passed the test.

□ She studied hard so, she passed the test.

4.23) Where should the semicolon be placed in this sentence: 'He wanted to go swimming the pool was closed'?

□ He;

□ pool;

□ closed;

□ swimming;

4.24) Which sentence correctly uses a colon?

□ There are three: primary colors red, blue, and yellow.

□ There are three primary colors red, blue: and yellow.

□ There are three primary colors: red, blue, and yellow.

□ There are: three primary colors red, blue, and yellow.

4.25) Which sentence correctly uses parentheses?

□ My mother who loves (gardening) planted new flowers.

□ My mother (who loves gardening planted new) flowers.

□ My mother (who loves gardening) planted new flowers.

□ My mother (who loves gardening) planted new flowers).

4.26) Where should the quotation marks be placed in this sentence: 'The teacher said, Please sit down.'?

□ 'The teacher said, Please sit down.'

□ The teacher said, Please sit down.'

□ The 'teacher said, Please sit down.'

□ The teacher said, 'Please sit down.'

4.27) Which sentence correctly uses a comma after an introductory phrase?

□ Before, the movie starts let's get some popcorn.

□ Before the movie starts, let's get some popcorn.

□ Before the movie starts let's get, some popcorn.

□ Before the movie starts let's, get some popcorn.

4.28) Which sentence avoids a fragment?

□ Since it was raining we canceled. The picnic.

□ Since it was raining, we canceled the picnic.

□ Since it was raining. We canceled the picnic.

□ Since it was raining. Canceled the picnic.

4.29) Where should the commas be placed in this sentence: 'She likes apples oranges and bananas'?

☐ She, likes apples oranges, and bananas.

☐ She likes apples, oranges, and bananas.

☐ She likes, apples oranges and, bananas.

☐ She likes apples oranges, and bananas.

4.30) Which sentence correctly uses a semicolon?

☐ We went; to the beach then we had dinner at a restaurant.

☐ We went to the beach; then, we had dinner at a restaurant.

☐ We went to the beach, then we had dinner at a restaurant.

☐ We went to the beach; then we had dinner at a restaurant.

4.31) Which sentence uses commas correctly?

☐ While I was studying, my friend called.

☐ While I was studying my friend called.

☐ While I was studying my friend, called.

☐ While I, was studying my friend called.

4.32) Which sentence avoids a comma splice?

☐ The sun set, and the stars appeared.

☐ The sun set and, the stars appeared.

☐ The sun set, the stars appeared.

☐ The sun, set and the stars appeared.

4.33) Where should the semicolon be placed in this sentence: 'The cake was delicious everyone wanted a second piece'?

☐ cake;

☐ piece;

☐ delicious;

☐ everyone;

4.34) Which sentence correctly uses a colon?

☐ He has: three pets a dog, a cat, and a hamster.

☐ He has three: pets a dog, a cat, and a hamster.

☐ He has three pets a dog, a cat: and a hamster.

☐ He has three pets: a dog, a cat, and a hamster.

4.35) Which sentence correctly uses parentheses?

☐ The concert (which was sold out was amazing).

☐ The concert (which was sold out) was amazing).

☐ The concert which was (sold out) was amazing.

☐ The concert (which was sold out) was amazing.

4.36) Where should the quotation marks be placed in this sentence: 'Can you believe it's already December?' he asked.

☐ Can 'you believe it's already December?' he asked.

☐ 'Can you believe it's already December?' he asked.

☐ Can you believe it's already December?' he asked.

☐ Can you 'believe it's already December?' he asked.

4.37) Which sentence correctly uses a comma after an introductory phrase?

☐ Because, it was late we decided to go home.

☐ Because it was late we decided to go, home.

☐ Because it was late we, decided to go home.

☐ Because it was late, we decided to go home.

4.38) Which sentence avoids a fragment?

☐ After the meeting ended. We discussed our plans.

☐ After the meeting ended, we discussed our plans.

☐ After the meeting ended we discussed. Our plans.

☐ After the meeting ended. Discussed our plans.

4.39) Where should the commas be placed in this sentence: 'I need paper pencils and erasers'?

☐ I need, paper pencils and, erasers.

☐ I need paper, pencils, and erasers.

☐ I need paper pencils, and erasers.

☐ I, need paper pencils, and erasers.

4.40) Which sentence correctly uses a semicolon?

☐ She finished her homework; then she went for a walk.

☐ She finished her homework, then she went for a walk.

☐ She finished her homework; then, she went for a walk.

☐ She finished; her homework then she went for a walk.

Topic 4 - Answers

Question Number	Answer	Explanation
4.1	After dinner, we went to the movies.	This sentence uses commas correctly.
4.2	I went to the store, and I bought some milk.	This sentence avoids a comma splice.
4.3	tomorrow;	The semicolon should be placed after "tomorrow".
4.4	I need the following items: milk, eggs, and bread.	This sentence correctly uses a colon.
4.5	My brother (who is a year older than me) is very tall.	This sentence correctly uses parentheses.
4.6	She said, 'I can't believe it's already Friday!'	This sentence correctly places the quotation marks.
4.7	After the movie, we went out for ice cream.	This sentence correctly uses a comma after an introductory phrase.
4.8	Because I was tired, I went to bed early.	This sentence avoids a fragment.
4.9	During the summer, we like to swim, fish, and hike.	This sentence correctly places the commas.
4.10	I have a test tomorrow; I can't go out tonight.	This sentence correctly uses a semicolon.
4.11	Before leaving, the kids cleaned their rooms.	This sentence uses commas correctly.
4.12	She loves to read, and she visits the library often.	This sentence avoids a comma splice.
4.13	house;	The semicolon should be placed after "house".
4.14	Remember to bring: your notebook, a pen, and a calculator.	This sentence correctly uses a colon.
4.15	The author (who wrote the famous series) will be signing books.	This sentence correctly uses parentheses.
4.16	He shouted, 'Watch out!'	This sentence correctly places the quotation marks.
4.17	In the morning, we will start the hike.	This sentence correctly uses a comma after an introductory phrase.
4.18	When I finished my homework, I went to bed.	This sentence avoids a fragment.

4.19	For dinner, we had steak, potatoes, and salad.	This sentence correctly places the commas.
4.20	We wanted to go to the park; however, it started to rain.	This sentence correctly uses a semicolon.
4.21	On our trip, we visited Paris, London, and Rome.	This sentence uses commas correctly.
4.22	She studied hard, so she passed the test.	This sentence avoids a comma splice.
4.23	swimming;	The semicolon should be placed after "swimming".
4.24	There are three primary colors: red, blue, and yellow.	This sentence correctly uses a colon.
4.25	My mother (who loves gardening) planted new flowers.	This sentence correctly uses parentheses.
4.26	The teacher said, 'Please sit down.'	This sentence correctly places the quotation marks.
4.27	Before the movie starts, let's get some popcorn.	This sentence correctly uses a comma after an introductory phrase.
4.28	Since it was raining, we canceled the picnic.	This sentence avoids a fragment.
4.29	She likes apples, oranges, and bananas.	This sentence correctly places the commas.
4.30	We went to the beach; then we had dinner at a restaurant.	This sentence correctly uses a semicolon.
4.31	While I was studying, my friend called.	This sentence uses commas correctly.
4.32	The sun set, and the stars appeared.	This sentence avoids a comma splice.
4.33	delicious;	The semicolon should be placed after "delicious".
4.34	He has three pets: a dog, a cat, and a hamster.	This sentence correctly uses a colon.
4.35	The concert (which was sold out) was amazing.	This sentence correctly uses parentheses.
4.36	'Can you believe it's already December?' he asked.	This sentence correctly places the quotation marks.
4.37	Because it was late, we decided to go home.	This sentence correctly uses a comma after an introductory phrase.
4.38	After the meeting ended, we discussed our plans.	This sentence avoids a fragment.
4.39	I need paper, pencils, and erasers.	This sentence correctly places the commas.
4.40	She finished her homework; then she went for a walk.	This sentence correctly uses a semicolon.

Topic 5 - Word Meaning

5.1) What does 'obsolete' mean?

☐ Popular

☐ New

☐ Common

☐ No longer in use

5.2) What does 'tumultuous' mean?

☐ Predictable

☐ Quiet

☐ Calm

☐ Chaotic

5.3) What does 'perseverance' mean?

☐ Persistent effort

☐ Laziness

☐ Giving up

☐ Immediate success

5.4) What does 'voracious' mean?

☐ Not hungry

☐ Selective

☐ Indifferent

☐ Eager to consume a lot

5.5) What does 'impartial' mean?

☐ Unfair

☐ Biased

☐ Unbiased

☐ Subjective

5.6) What does 'ebullient' mean?

☐ Tired

☐ Sad

☐ Cheerful and full of energy

☐ Calm

5.7) What does 'cacophony' mean?

☐ Melody

☐ Harsh noise

☐ Silence

☐ Harmony

5.8) What does 'ephemeral' mean?

☐ Short-lived

☐ Eternal

☐ Permanent

☐ Long-lasting

5.9) What does 'disdain' mean?

☐ Respect

☐ Approval

☐ Lack of respect

☐ Admiration

5.10) What does 'ostentatious' mean?

☐ Plain

☐ Modest

☐ Simple

☐ Showy

5.11) What does 'malevolent' mean?

☐ Happy

☐ Generous

☐ Kind

☐ Evil

5.12) What does 'ubiquitous' mean?

☐ Unique

☐ Uncommon

☐ Rare

☐ Everywhere

5.13) What does 'garrulous' mean?

☐ Quiet

☐ Silent

☐ Talkative

☐ Reserved

5.14) What does 'insatiable' mean?

☐ Easily satisfied

☐ Uninterested

☐ Content

☐ Impossible to satisfy

5.15) What does 'nefarious' mean?

☐ Innocent

☐ Good

☐ Honest

☐ Wicked

5.16) What does 'benevolent' mean?

☐ Indifferent

☐ Mean

☐ Kind

☐ Cruel

5.17) What does 'aloof' mean?

☐ Friendly

☐ Welcoming

☐ Distant

☐ Warm

5.18) What does 'sagacious' mean?

☐ Unwise

☐ Ignorant

☐ Foolish

☐ Wise

5.19) What does 'acrimonious' mean?

☐ Bitter

☐ Pleasant

☐ Friendly

☐ Sweet

5.20) What does 'clandestine' mean?

☐ Secretive

☐ Open

☐ Obvious

☐ Public

5.21) What does 'sycophant' mean?

□ Flatterer

□ Leader

□ Worker

□ Critic

5.22) What does 'languid' mean?

□ Busy

□ Energetic

□ Slow and relaxed

□ Active

5.23) What does 'perfunctory' mean?

□ Done without care

□ Careful

□ Thorough

□ Meticulous

5.24) What does 'copious' mean?

□ Limited

□ Abundant

□ Few

□ Scarce

5.25) What does 'ameliorate' mean?

☐ Destroy

☐ Worsen

☐ Improve

☐ Neglect

5.26) What does 'incongruous' mean?

☐ Appropriate

☐ Suitable

☐ Out of place

☐ Fitting

5.27) What does 'vicarious' mean?

☐ Personal

☐ Firsthand

☐ Direct

☐ Experienced through another

5.28) What does 'proclivity' mean?

☐ Aversion

☐ Tendency

☐ Repulsion

☐ Dislike

5.29) What does 'aplomb' mean?

☐ Fear

☐ Confidence

☐ Hesitation

☐ Doubt

5.30) What does 'incorrigible' mean?

☐ Changeable

☐ Teachable

☐ Not able to be corrected

☐ Malleable

5.31) What does 'ambivalent' mean?

☐ Determined

☐ Certain

☐ Having mixed feelings

☐ Confident

5.32) What does 'recalcitrant' mean?

☐ Willing

☐ Agreeable

☐ Stubbornly resistant

☐ Obedient

5.33) What does 'assiduous' mean?

☐ Lazy

☐ Idle

☐ Hardworking

☐ Negligent

5.34) What does 'esoteric' mean?

☐ Understood by few

☐ Common

☐ Widespread

☐ Popular

5.35) What does 'reticent' mean?

☐ Reserved

☐ Garrulous

☐ Outgoing

☐ Talkative

5.36) What does 'ineffable' mean?

☐ Articulate

☐ Expressible

☐ Too great to be expressed in words

☐ Describable

5.37) What does 'abscond' mean?

☐ To appear

☐ To run away secretly

☐ To arrive

☐ To stay

5.38) What does 'idiosyncrasy' mean?

☐ A usual feature

☐ A peculiar trait

☐ A standard characteristic

☐ A common trait

5.39) What does 'mellifluous' mean?

☐ Unpleasant

☐ Sweet sounding

☐ Cacophonous

☐ Harsh

5.40) What does 'tenacious' mean?

☐ Yielding

☐ Weak

☐ Persistent

☐ Relenting

ALEXANDER-GRACE EDUCATION

Topic 5 - Answers

Question Number	Answer	Explanation
5.1	No longer in use	"Obsolete" means no longer in use.
5.2	Chaotic	"Tumultuous" means chaotic.
5.3	Persistent effort	"Perseverance" means persistent effort.
5.4	Eager to consume a lot	"Voracious" means eager to consume a lot.
5.5	Unbiased	"Impartial" means unbiased.
5.6	Cheerful and full of energy	"Ebullient" means cheerful and full of energy.
5.7	Harsh noise	"Cacophony" means harsh noise.
5.8	Short-lived	"Ephemeral" means short-lived.
5.9	Lack of respect	"Disdain" means lack of respect.
5.10	Showy	"Ostentatious" means showy.
5.11	Evil	"Malevolent" means evil.
5.12	Everywhere	"Ubiquitous" means everywhere.
5.13	Talkative	"Garrulous" means talkative.
5.14	Impossible to satisfy	"Insatiable" means impossible to satisfy.
5.15	Wicked	"Nefarious" means wicked.
5.16	Kind	"Benevolent" means kind.
5.17	Distant	"Aloof" means distant.
5.18	Wise	"Sagacious" means wise.

5.19	Bitter	"Acrimonious" means bitter.
5.20	Secretive	"Clandestine" means secretive.
5.21	Flatterer	"Sycophant" means flatterer.
5.22	Slow and relaxed	"Languid" means slow and relaxed.
5.23	Done without care	"Perfunctory" means done without care.
5.24	Abundant	"Copious" means abundant.
5.25	Improve	"Ameliorate" means improve.
5.26	Out of place	"Incongruous" means out of place.
5.27	Experienced through another	"Vicarious" means experienced through another.
5.28	Tendency	"Proclivity" means tendency.
5.29	Confidence	"Aplomb" means confidence.
5.30	Not able to be corrected	"Incorrigible" means not able to be corrected.
5.31	Having mixed feelings	"Ambivalent" means having mixed feelings.
5.32	Stubbornly resistant	"Recalcitrant" means stubbornly resistant.
5.33	Hardworking	"Assiduous" means hardworking.
5.34	Understood by few	"Esoteric" means understood by few.
5.35	Reserved	"Reticent" means reserved.
5.36	Too great to be expressed in words	"Ineffable" means too great to be expressed in words.
5.37	To run away secretly	"Abscond" means to run away secretly.
5.38	A peculiar trait	"Idiosyncrasy" means a peculiar trait.
5.39	Sweet sounding	"Mellifluous" means sweet sounding.
5.40	Persistent	"Tenacious" means persistent.

Topic 6 – Spelling

6.1) How do you spell the word meaning 'to enliven or invigorate'?

☐ Exilerate

☐ Exhilerate

☐ Exhilarat

☐ Exhilarate

6.2) How do you spell the word meaning 'the act of preserving or keeping in good condition'?

☐ Maintanence

☐ Maintenance

☐ Maintenence

☐ Maintainance

6.3) How do you spell the word meaning 'to accept something reluctantly but without protest'?

☐ Aquiesce

☐ Acquies

☐ Acquise

☐ Acquiesce

6.4) How do you spell the word meaning 'a system of government in which most of the important decisions are made by state officials'?

☐ Bureaucrasy

☐ Bureaucracy

☐ Beaurocracy

☐ Beurocracy

6.5) How do you spell the word meaning 'an expert judge in matters of taste'?

☐ Conoissur

☐ Connoisseur

☐ Conoisseur

☐ Connesseur

6.6) How do you spell the word meaning 'the part of the mind that tells you certain actions are right or wrong'?

☐ Consience

☐ Concience

☐ Conscience

☐ Consciense

6.7) How do you spell the word meaning 'to feel self-conscious distress'?

☐ Embarass

☐ Embarras

☐ Embarrass

☐ Embaras

6.8) How do you spell the word meaning 'a scale of temperature'?

☐ Fahrenheit

☐ Fahranheit

☐ Fahrenheit

☐ Farenheit

6.9) How do you spell the word meaning 'to measure precisely'?

☐ Gage

☐ Guage

☐ Gauge

☐ Gouge

6.10) How do you spell the word meaning 'a system or organization in which people or groups are ranked one above the other'?

☐ Heirarchy

☐ Hierarchy

☐ Hierarcy

☐ Heirarcy

6.11) How do you spell the word meaning 'absolutely necessary'?

☐ Indespensible

☐ Indispensible

☐ Indispensable

☐ Indispensabel

6.12) How do you spell the word meaning 'danger or risk'?

☐ Jeapardy

☐ Jepardy

☐ Jeopardy

☐ Jeapordy

6.13) How do you spell the word meaning 'a special skill or talent'?

☐ Nack

☐ Knac

☐ Knakk

☐ Knack

6.14) How do you spell the word meaning 'a person who acts as a link to assist communication or cooperation'?

☐ Leaison

☐ Liaison

☐ Laison

☐ Liason

6.15) How do you spell the word meaning 'a movement or series of moves requiring skill and care'?

☐ Maneuver

☐ Maneuver

☐ Maneuver

☐ Maneuver

6.16) How do you spell the word meaning 'the fact of being required or indispensable'?

☐ Nessessity

☐ Necesity

☐ Necesity

☐ Necessity

6.17) How do you spell the word meaning 'extremely unpleasant'?

☐ Obnoxious

☐ Obnoxous

☐ Obnoxius

☐ Obnoxtious

6.18) How do you spell the word meaning 'the highest legislature in a country'?

☐ Parliment

☐ Parliment

☐ Parliament

☐ Parlament

6.19) How do you spell the word meaning 'a set of printed or written questions with a choice of answers'?

☐ Questionair

☐ Questionnair

☐ Questionnaire

☐ Questionaire

6.20) How do you spell the word meaning 'to make someone or something look or feel younger, fresher, or more lively'?

☐ Rejuvenate

☐ Rejuvenete

☐ Rejuvinate

☐ Rejuvinate

6.21) How do you spell the word meaning 'a representation of the outline of an object filled in with a solid color'?

☐ Silouette

☐ Sillhouette

☐ Silhuette

☐ Silhouette

6.22) How do you spell the word meaning 'close observation, especially of a suspected spy or criminal'?

☐ Surveilance

☐ Survaillance

☐ Surveillance

☐ Surveylance

6.23) How do you spell the word meaning 'a strip of wood, metal, or stone forming the bottom of a doorway'?

☐ Thresold

☐ Threashold

☐ Threshhold

☐ Threshold

6.24) How do you spell the word meaning 'fully in agreement'?

☐ Unanimous

☐ Unanimuos

☐ Unanamous

☐ Unanimus

6.25) How do you spell the word meaning 'punishment inflicted or retribution exacted for an injury or wrong'?

☐ Vengance

☐ Vengence

☐ Vengeance

☐ Vengence

6.26) How do you spell the word meaning 'strange or mysterious, especially in an unsettling way'?

☐ Wierd

☐ Weird

☐ Weerd

☐ Weird

6.27) How do you spell the word meaning 'a musical instrument with wooden bars'?

☐ Xylofone

☐ Xylophone

☐ Xylofhone

☐ Zylophone

6.28) How do you spell the word meaning 'a gentle, mild breeze'?

☐ Zefir

☐ Zefer

☐ Zefyr

☐ Zephyr

6.29) How do you spell the word meaning 'concerned with beauty or the appreciation of beauty'?

☐ Aesthetik

☐ Aesthetic

☐ Aestetick

☐ Esthetic

6.30) How do you spell the word meaning 'a vegetable with dense green or purple flower heads'?

☐ Brocolli

☐ Brocili

☐ Brocolli

☐ Broccoli

6.31) How do you spell the word meaning 'mutual trust and friendship among people who spend a lot of time together'?

☐ Camaraderie

☐ Camaradarie

☐ Comraderie

☐ Camaraderie

6.32) How do you spell the word meaning 'to mislead or falsely persuade others'?

☐ Deceive

☐ Deceve

☐ Decieve

☐ Deceeve

6.33) How do you spell the word meaning 'a person who organizes and operates a business'?

☐ Entrepreneur

☐ Entreprener

☐ Entreprenuer

☐ Entrepeneur

6.34) How do you spell the word meaning 'a bright purplish-red color'?

☐ Fuchisia

☐ Fuschia

☐ Fuchia

☐ Fuchsia

6.35) How do you spell the word meaning 'uncalled for or lacking good reason'?

☐ Gratious

☐ Gratitious

☐ Gratuitous

☐ Gratuitos

6.36) How do you spell the word meaning 'to disturb persistently'?

☐ Harrass

☐ Harrass

☐ Harass

☐ Haras

6.37) How do you spell the word meaning 'to implant a disease agent in a person, animal, or plant'?

☐ Innoculate

☐ Innaculate

☐ Inoculate

☐ Inoculate

6.38) How do you spell the word meaning 'the act or an instance of placing two or more things side by side'?

☐ Juxstaposition

☐ Juxtiposition

☐ Juxtaposition

☐ Juxstaposition

6.39) How do you spell the word meaning 'intelligent and well-informed'?

□ Knowldgeable

□ Knowledgeable

□ Knowledgable

□ Knowledgable

6.40) How do you spell the word meaning 'extremely elegant and comfortable'?

□ Luxoriuos

□ Luxurous

□ Luxurious

□ Luxurios

Topic 6 - Answers

Question Number	Answer	Explanation
6.1	Exhilarate	The correct spelling for the word meaning 'to enliven or invigorate' is "Exhilarate".
6.2	Maintenance	The correct spelling for the word meaning 'the act of preserving or keeping in good condition' is "Maintenance".
6.3	Acquiesce	The correct spelling for the word meaning 'to accept something reluctantly but without protest' is "Acquiesce".
6.4	Bureaucracy	The correct spelling for the word meaning 'a system of government in which most of the important decisions are made by state officials' is "Bureaucracy".
6.5	Connoisseur	The correct spelling for the word meaning 'an expert judge in matters of taste' is "Connoisseur".
6.6	Conscience	The correct spelling for the word meaning 'the part of the mind that tells you certain actions are right or wrong' is "Conscience".
6.7	Embarrass	The correct spelling for the word meaning 'to feel self-conscious distress' is "Embarrass".
6.8	Fahrenheit	The correct spelling for the word meaning 'a scale of temperature' is "Fahrenheit".
6.9	Gauge	The correct spelling for the word meaning 'to measure precisely' is "Gauge".
6.10	Hierarchy	The correct spelling for the word meaning 'a system or organization in which people or groups are ranked one above the other' is "Hierarchy".
6.11	Indispensable	The correct spelling for the word meaning 'absolutely necessary' is "Indispensable".
6.12	Jeopardy	The correct spelling for the word meaning 'danger or risk' is "Jeopardy".
6.13	Knack	The correct spelling for the word meaning 'a special skill or talent' is "Knack".
6.14	Liaison	The correct spelling for the word meaning 'a person who acts as a link to assist communication or cooperation' is "Liaison".
6.15	Maneuver	The correct spelling for the word meaning 'a movement or series of moves requiring skill and care' is "Maneuver".
6.16	Necessity	The correct spelling for the word meaning 'the fact of being required or indispensable' is "Necessity".
6.17	Obnoxious	The correct spelling for the word meaning 'extremely unpleasant' is "Obnoxious".
6.18	Parliament	The correct spelling for the word meaning 'the highest legislature in a country' is "Parliament".

6.19	Questionnaire	The correct spelling for the word meaning 'a set of printed or written questions with a choice of answers' is "Questionnaire".
6.20	Rejuvenate	The correct spelling for the word meaning 'to make someone or something look or feel younger, fresher, or more lively' is "Rejuvenate".
6.21	Silhouette	The correct spelling for the word meaning 'a representation of the outline of an object filled in with a solid color' is "Silhouette".
6.22	Surveillance	The correct spelling for the word meaning 'close observation, especially of a suspected spy or criminal' is "Surveillance".
6.23	Threshold	The correct spelling for the word meaning 'a strip of wood, metal, or stone forming the bottom of a doorway' is "Threshold".
6.24	Unanimous	The correct spelling for the word meaning 'fully in agreement' is "Unanimous".
6.25	Vengeance	The correct spelling for the word meaning 'punishment inflicted or retribution exacted for an injury or wrong' is "Vengeance".
6.26	Weird	The correct spelling for the word meaning 'strange or mysterious, especially in an unsettling way' is "Weird".
6.27	Xylophone	The correct spelling for the word meaning 'a musical instrument with wooden bars' is "Xylophone".
6.28	Zephyr	The correct spelling for the word meaning 'a gentle, mild breeze' is "Zephyr".
6.29	Aesthetic	The correct spelling for the word meaning 'concerned with beauty or the appreciation of beauty' is "Aesthetic".
6.30	Broccoli	The correct spelling for the word meaning 'a vegetable with dense green or purple flower heads' is "Broccoli".
6.31	Camaraderie	The correct spelling for the word meaning 'mutual trust and friendship among people who spend a lot of time together' is "Camaraderie".
6.32	Deceive	The correct spelling for the word meaning 'to mislead or falsely persuade others' is "Deceive".
6.33	Entrepreneur	The correct spelling for the word meaning 'a person who organizes and operates a business' is "Entrepreneur".
6.34	Fuchsia	The correct spelling for the word meaning 'a bright purplish-red color' is "Fuchsia".
6.35	Gratuitous	The correct spelling for the word meaning 'uncalled for or lacking good reason' is "Gratuitous".
6.36	Harass	The correct spelling for the word meaning 'to disturb persistently' is "Harass".
6.37	Inoculate	The correct spelling for the word meaning 'to implant a disease agent in a person, animal, or plant' is "Inoculate".
6.38	Juxtaposition	The correct spelling for the word meaning 'the act or an instance of placing two or more things side by side' is "Juxtaposition".
6.39	Knowledgeable	The correct spelling for the word meaning 'intelligent and well-informed' is "Knowledgeable".
6.40	Luxurious	The correct spelling for the word meaning 'extremely elegant and comfortable' is "Luxurious".

Topic 7 – Syntax and Parallelism

7.1) Identify the sentence that maintains consistent verb tense.

☐ She likes to swim and running.

☐ She likes swimming and ran.

☐ She liked to swim and running.

☐ She likes to swim and to run.

7.2) Which sentence demonstrates correct parallel structure?

☐ The coach said we should run quickly, play aggressively, and we should have fun.

☐ The coach said we should run quickly, play aggressively, and we should have funning.

☐ The coach said we should run quickly, play aggressively, and have fun.

☐ The coach said we should run quickly, to play aggressively, and having fun.

7.3) Identify the sentence that correctly avoids a misplaced or dangling modifier.

☐ Walking through the park, the flowers were in full bloom.

☐ In full bloom, we walked through the park and saw the flowers.

☐ We saw walking through the park, flowers in full bloom.

☐ Walking through the park, we saw flowers in full bloom.

7.4) Choose the sentence that demonstrates correct parallelism.

☐ She enjoys reading, writing, and painting.

☐ She enjoys to read, writing, and painting.

☐ She enjoys reading, writing, and to paint.

☐ She enjoys reading, writing, and paint.

7.5) Which sentence maintains a consistent verb tense?

☐ Yesterday, he walked to the store and buys some milk.

☐ Yesterday, he walked to the store and bought some milk.

☐ Yesterday, he walking to the store and bought some milk.

☐ Yesterday, he walks to the store and buys some milk.

7.6) Identify the sentence that avoids a dangling modifier.

☐ The movie was disappointing after reading the book.

☐ The book was read, and then the movie was disappointing.

☐ After reading the book, we found the movie disappointing.

☐ After reading the book, the movie was disappointing.

7.7) Which sentence demonstrates correct parallel structure?

☐ The job requires attention to detail, the ability to work quickly, and reliability.

☐ The job requires attention to detail, the ability to work quickly, and you must be reliable.

☐ The job requires attention to detail, working quickly, and to be reliable.

☐ The job requires attention to detail, the ability to work quickly, and being reliable.

7.8) Choose the sentence that maintains consistent verb tense.

☐ She sang while he plays the piano.

☐ She was singing while he played the piano.

☐ She sings while he played the piano.

☐ She was singing while he plays the piano.

7.9) Identify the sentence that avoids a misplaced modifier.

□ Almost, we ate all the cookies.

□ We almost ate all the cookies.

□ We ate all the cookies almost.

□ We ate almost all the cookies.

7.10) Which sentence demonstrates correct parallel structure?

□ He likes hiking, to swim, and biking.

□ He likes to hike, swimming, and to bike.

□ He likes hiking, swimming, and biking.

□ He likes to hike, to swim, and biking.

7.11) Identify the sentence that maintains consistent verb tense.

□ He finished his homework and then played video games.

□ He finishing his homework and then played video games.

□ He finishes his homework and then played video games.

□ He finished his homework and then plays video games.

7.12) Which sentence demonstrates correct parallel structure?

□ She likes to jog, to swim, and biking.

□ She likes jogging, swimming, and biking.

□ She likes to jog, swimming, and to bike.

□ She likes jogging, to swim, and biking.

7.13) Identify the sentence that correctly avoids a misplaced or dangling modifier.

□ While eating lunch, the phone rang.

□ While we were eating lunch, the phone rang.

□ Eating lunch, the phone rang.

□ The phone rang while eating lunch.

7.14) Choose the sentence that demonstrates correct parallelism.

□ The teacher said to study hard, to complete all assignments, and you should get enough rest.

□ The teacher said to study hard, to complete all assignments, and getting enough rest.

□ The teacher said to study hard, to complete all assignments, and to get enough rest.

□ The teacher said to study hard, completing all assignments, and you should get enough rest.

7.15) Which sentence maintains a consistent verb tense?

□ Last night, she watches TV and talked on the phone.

□ Last night, she watched TV and talks on the phone.

□ Last night, she watched TV and talked on the phone.

□ Last night, she watches TV and talking on the phone.

7.16) Identify the sentence that avoids a dangling modifier.

□ The view was beautiful hiking up the mountain.

□ Hiking up the mountain, we enjoyed the beautiful view.

□ Hiking up the mountain, the view was enjoyed.

□ Hiking up the mountain, the view was beautiful.

7.17) Which sentence demonstrates correct parallel structure?

☐ The recipe calls for chopping onions, slicing tomatoes, and to grate cheese.

☐ The recipe calls for chopping onions, slicing tomatoes, and grating cheese.

☐ The recipe calls for chopping onions, slice tomatoes, and grating cheese.

☐ The recipe calls for chopping onions, slicing tomatoes, and grated cheese.

7.18) Choose the sentence that maintains consistent verb tense.

☐ During the summer, he swam every day and plays soccer.

☐ During the summer, he swims every day and plays soccer.

☐ During the summer, he swam every day and played soccer.

☐ During the summer, he swims every day and played soccer.

7.19) Identify the sentence that avoids a misplaced modifier.

☐ We almost watched the movie for two hours.

☐ We watched the movie almost for two hours.

☐ We watched the movie for almost two hours.

☐ We watched almost the movie for two hours.

7.20) Which sentence demonstrates correct parallel structure?

☐ She wants to learn to cook, sewing, and to paint.

☐ She wants to learn how to cook, to sew, and painting.

☐ She wants to learn how to cook, to sew, and to paint.

☐ She wants to learn cooking, sewing, and to paint.

7.21) Identify the sentence that maintains consistent verb tense.

☐ She completed her project and then celebrated with friends.

☐ She completed her project and then celebrates with friends.

☐ She completing her project and then celebrated with friends.

☐ She completes her project and then celebrated with friends.

7.22) Which sentence demonstrates correct parallel structure?

☐ He likes to fish, to hunt, and hiking.

☐ He likes fishing, to hunt, and hiking.

☐ He likes to fish, hunting, and to hike.

☐ He likes fishing, hunting, and hiking.

7.23) Identify the sentence that correctly avoids a misplaced or dangling modifier.

☐ The car broke down driving to work.

☐ While driving to work, the car broke down.

☐ While he was driving to work, the car broke down.

☐ Driving to work, the car broke down.

7.24) Choose the sentence that demonstrates correct parallelism.

☐ The job requires skill, dedication, and punctuality.

☐ The job requires skill, dedication, and being punctual.

☐ The job requires skill, to be dedicated, and punctual.

☐ The job requires skill, dedication, and you must be punctual.

7.25) Which sentence maintains a consistent verb tense?

☐ Last weekend, we visited the museum and ate at a nice restaurant.

☐ Last weekend, we visit the museum and ate at a nice restaurant.

☐ Last weekend, we visited the museum and eat at a nice restaurant.

☐ Last weekend, we visit the museum and eating at a nice restaurant.

7.26) Identify the sentence that avoids a dangling modifier.

☐ Walking along the beach, the sunset was beautiful.

☐ The sunset was beautiful walking along the beach.

☐ Walking along the beach, the sunset was enjoyed.

☐ Walking along the beach, we enjoyed the beautiful sunset.

7.27) Which sentence demonstrates correct parallel structure?

☐ To succeed, you need to work hard, be honest, and never giving up.

☐ To succeed, you need to work hard, be honest, and never give up.

☐ To succeed, you need to work hard, being honest, and never give up.

☐ To succeed, you need to work hard, be honest, and not give up.

7.28) Choose the sentence that maintains consistent verb tense.

☐ In the fall, the leaves changed color and fall from the trees.

☐ In the fall, the leaves changed color and fell from the trees.

☐ In the fall, the leaves change color and fall from the trees.

☐ In the fall, the leaves change color and fallen from the trees.

7.29) Identify the sentence that avoids a misplaced modifier.

☐ We barely heard the speaker for entire the lecture.

☐ We heard barely the speaker for the entire lecture.

☐ We barely heard the speaker for the entire lecture.

☐ We heard the speaker barely for the entire lecture.

7.30) Which sentence demonstrates correct parallel structure?

☐ The book was interesting, informative, and enjoyable.

☐ The book was interesting, informative, and to enjoy.

☐ The book was interesting, informative, and it was a joy.

☐ The book was interesting, informative, and it was enjoyable.

7.31) Identify the sentence that maintains consistent verb tense.

☐ She practiced the piano every day and performs in the recital.

☐ She practices the piano every day and performed in the recital.

☐ She practices the piano every day and performs in the recital.

☐ She practiced the piano every day and performed in the recital.

7.32) Which sentence demonstrates correct parallel structure?

☐ The team needs training hard, eating well, and to get enough rest.

☐ The team needs to train hard, eat well, and getting enough rest.

☐ The team needs to train hard, eat well, and get enough rest.

☐ The team needs to train hard, eating well, and get enough rest.

7.33) Identify the sentence that correctly avoids a misplaced or dangling modifier.

☐ While we were reading the book, the plot was confusing.

☐ While reading the book, the plot was confusing.

☐ The plot was confusing while reading the book.

☐ Reading the book, the plot was confusing.

7.34) Choose the sentence that demonstrates correct parallelism.

☐ To be successful, you must be disciplined, motivating, and willing to work hard.

☐ To be successful, you must be disciplined, motivated, and willing to work hard.

☐ To be successful, you must be disciplined, motivated, and working hard.

☐ To be successful, you must be disciplined, motivated, and hard working.

7.35) Which sentence maintains a consistent verb tense?

☐ Every morning, she ran five miles and drank a protein shake.

☐ Every morning, she runs five miles and drank a protein shake.

☐ Every morning, she runs five miles and drinks a protein shake.

☐ Every morning, she ran five miles and drinks a protein shake.

7.36) Identify the sentence that avoids a dangling modifier.

☐ Looking through the telescope, the stars were bright.

☐ Looking through the telescope, we saw the bright stars.

☐ The stars were bright looking through the telescope.

☐ Looking through the telescope, the stars were seen.

7.37) Which sentence demonstrates correct parallel structure?

☐ The conference will cover new strategies, innovative techniques, and future trend.

☐ The conference will cover new strategies, innovative techniques, and future trends.

☐ The conference will cover new strategies, innovating techniques, and future trends.

☐ The conference will cover new strategies, innovative techniques, and future trending.

7.38) Choose the sentence that maintains consistent verb tense.

☐ He studied for the exam and then went to bed early.

☐ He studies for the exam and then went to bed early.

☐ He studied for the exam and then goes to bed early.

☐ He studies for the exam and then goes to bed early.

7.39) Identify the sentence that avoids a misplaced modifier.

☐ Almost, we finished the project in two weeks.

☐ We finished almost the project in two weeks.

☐ We finished the project almost in two weeks.

☐ We almost finished the project in two weeks.

7.40) Which sentence demonstrates correct parallel structure?

☐ The athlete needs to build strength, improve endurance, and increase speed.

☐ The athlete needs to build strength, improving endurance, and increase speed.

☐ The athlete needs to build strength, improve endurance, and increasing speed.

☐ The athlete needs to build strength, improve endurance, and increased speed.

Topic 7 - Answers

Question Number	Answer	Explanation
7.1	She likes to swim and to run.	This sentence maintains consistent verb tense.
7.2	The coach said we should run quickly, play aggressively, and have fun.	This sentence demonstrates correct parallel structure.
7.3	Walking through the park, we saw flowers in full bloom.	This sentence correctly avoids a misplaced or dangling modifier.
7.4	She enjoys reading, writing, and painting.	This sentence demonstrates correct parallelism.
7.5	Yesterday, he walked to the store and bought some milk.	This sentence maintains a consistent verb tense.
7.6	After reading the book, we found the movie disappointing.	This sentence avoids a dangling modifier.
7.7	The job requires attention to detail, the ability to work quickly, and reliability.	This sentence demonstrates correct parallel structure.
7.8	She was singing while he played the piano.	This sentence maintains consistent verb tense.
7.9	We almost ate all the cookies.	This sentence avoids a misplaced modifier.
7.10	He likes hiking, swimming, and biking.	This sentence demonstrates correct parallel structure.
7.11	He finished his homework and then played video games.	This sentence maintains consistent verb tense.
7.12	She likes jogging, swimming, and biking.	This sentence demonstrates correct parallel structure.
7.13	While we were eating lunch, the phone rang.	This sentence correctly avoids a misplaced or dangling modifier.
7.14	The teacher said to study hard, to complete all assignments, and to get enough rest.	This sentence demonstrates correct parallelism.
7.15	Last night, she watched TV and talked on the phone.	This sentence maintains a consistent verb tense.
7.16	Hiking up the mountain, we enjoyed the beautiful view.	This sentence avoids a dangling modifier.
7.17	The recipe calls for chopping onions, slicing tomatoes, and grating cheese.	This sentence demonstrates correct parallel structure.
7.18	During the summer, he swam every day and played soccer.	This sentence maintains consistent verb tense.

7.19	We watched the movie for almost two hours.	This sentence avoids a misplaced modifier.
7.20	She wants to learn how to cook, to sew, and to paint.	This sentence demonstrates correct parallel structure.
7.21	She completed her project and then celebrated with friends.	This sentence maintains consistent verb tense.
7.22	He likes fishing, hunting, and hiking.	This sentence demonstrates correct parallel structure.
7.23	While he was driving to work, the car broke down.	This sentence correctly avoids a misplaced or dangling modifier.
7.24	The job requires skill, dedication, and punctuality.	This sentence demonstrates correct parallelism.
7.25	Last weekend, we visited the museum and ate at a nice restaurant.	This sentence maintains a consistent verb tense.
7.26	Walking along the beach, we enjoyed the beautiful sunset.	This sentence avoids a dangling modifier.
7.27	To succeed, you need to work hard, be honest, and never give up.	This sentence demonstrates correct parallel structure.
7.28	In the fall, the leaves changed color and fell from the trees.	This sentence maintains consistent verb tense.
7.29	We barely heard the speaker for the entire lecture.	This sentence avoids a misplaced modifier.
7.30	The book was interesting, informative, and enjoyable.	This sentence demonstrates correct parallel structure.
7.31	She practiced the piano every day and performed in the recital.	This sentence maintains consistent verb tense.
7.32	The team needs to train hard, eat well, and get enough rest.	This sentence demonstrates correct parallel structure.
7.33	While we were reading the book, the plot was confusing.	This sentence correctly avoids a misplaced or dangling modifier.
7.34	To be successful, you must be disciplined, motivated, and willing to work hard.	This sentence demonstrates correct parallelism.
7.35	Every morning, she ran five miles and drank a protein shake.	This sentence maintains a consistent verb tense.
7.36	Looking through the telescope, we saw the bright stars.	This sentence avoids a dangling modifier.
7.37	The conference will cover new strategies, innovative techniques, and future trends.	This sentence demonstrates correct parallel structure.
7.38	He studied for the exam and then went to bed early.	This sentence maintains consistent verb tense.
7.39	We almost finished the project in two weeks.	This sentence avoids a misplaced modifier.
7.40	The athlete needs to build strength, improve endurance, and increase speed.	This sentence demonstrates correct parallel structure.

Topic 8 – Definitions from Sentences

8.1) What does 'abscond' mean in the sentence: 'The thief decided to abscond with the stolen jewels'?

□ destroy

□ give away

□ hide

□ run away

8.2) What does 'benevolent' mean in the sentence: 'Her benevolent nature made her beloved by all'?

□ angry

□ kind

□ shy

□ cruel

8.3) What does 'cacophony' mean in the sentence: 'The band produced a cacophony of sound as they tuned their instruments'?

□ silence

□ melody

□ harsh noise

□ soft music

8.4) What does 'debilitate' mean in the sentence: 'The disease continued to debilitate the patient over time'?

☐ strengthen

☐ heal

☐ weaken

☐ comfort

8.5) What does 'ephemeral' mean in the sentence: 'The beauty of the sunset was ephemeral, lasting only a few moments'?

☐ endless

☐ ordinary

☐ short-lived

☐ noticeable

8.6) What does 'furtive' mean in the sentence: 'He took a furtive glance at the answers on his friend's paper'?

☐ bold

☐ secretive

☐ open

☐ honest

8.7) What does 'gregarious' mean in the sentence: 'She was a gregarious person who loved to be around others'?

☐ shy

☐ lazy

☐ quiet

☐ sociable

8.8) What does 'harbinger' mean in the sentence: 'The blooming flowers are a harbinger of spring'?

☐ end

☐ coincidence

☐ result

☐ sign

8.9) What does 'juxtapose' mean in the sentence: 'The artist chose to juxtapose bright colors with dark shades'?

☐ separate

☐ place side by side

☐ hide

☐ mix together

8.10) What does 'languid' mean in the sentence: 'The hot weather made everyone feel languid and tired'?

□ busy

□ slow and relaxed

□ active

□ energetic

8.11) What does 'mellifluous' mean in the sentence: 'Her mellifluous voice captivated the audience'?

□ sweet sounding

□ boring

□ harsh

□ loud

8.12) What does 'nebulous' mean in the sentence: 'His plans for the future were still quite nebulous'?

□ unclear

□ clear

□ detailed

□ simple

8.13) What does 'obfuscate' mean in the sentence: 'The politician tried to obfuscate the facts during the debate'?

□ simplify

□ reveal

□ clarify

□ confuse

8.14) What does 'pernicious' mean in the sentence: 'The pernicious effects of pollution are becoming more apparent'?

□ beneficial

□ neutral

□ harmful

□ invisible

8.15) What does 'quixotic' mean in the sentence: 'His quixotic quest for perfection left him constantly disappointed'?

□ idealistic

□ realistic

□ cynical

□ pessimistic

8.16) What does 'recalcitrant' mean in the sentence: 'The recalcitrant student refused to follow the teacher's instructions'?

☐ obedient

☐ attentive

☐ stubbornly resistant

☐ eager

8.17) What does 'sycophant' mean in the sentence: 'The sycophant constantly praised his boss to get ahead'?

☐ worker

☐ critic

☐ flatterer

☐ leader

8.18) What does 'tangible' mean in the sentence: 'The tension in the room was almost tangible'?

☐ invisible

☐ unimportant

☐ perceptible

☐ trivial

8.19) What does 'ubiquitous' mean in the sentence: 'Smartphones have become ubiquitous in today's society'?

☐ uncommon

☐ rare

☐ everywhere

☐ expensive

8.20) What does 'vicissitude' mean in the sentence: 'They remained friends through the vicissitudes of life'?

☐ changes

☐ joys

☐ simplicity

☐ predictability

8.21) What does 'wizened' mean in the sentence: 'The wizened old man shared stories of his youth'?

☐ wrinkled

☐ tall

☐ strong

☐ youthful

8.22) What does 'xenophobia' mean in the sentence: 'His xenophobia made him distrustful of foreigners'?

☐ interest in cultures

☐ love of travel

☐ fear of strangers

☐ fear of heights

8.23) What does 'zealous' mean in the sentence: 'She was zealous in her efforts to raise money for the charity'?

☐ uninterested

☐ enthusiastic

☐ lazy

☐ angry

8.24) What does 'acrimony' mean in the sentence: 'The acrimony between the two rivals was apparent to everyone'?

☐ indifference

☐ bitterness

☐ support

☐ friendliness

8.25) What does 'banal' mean in the sentence: 'The movie was filled with banal dialogue that was predictable and dull'?

☐ original

☐ unusual

☐ exciting

☐ trite

8.26) What does 'chagrin' mean in the sentence: 'Much to her chagrin, she realized she had forgotten her homework'?

☐ happiness

☐ excitement

☐ pride

☐ embarrassment

8.27) What does 'disparate' mean in the sentence: 'The group was composed of individuals with disparate backgrounds and experiences'?

☐ different

☐ common

☐ similar

☐ uniform

8.28) What does 'enigma' mean in the sentence: 'The origin of the ancient artifact remains an enigma'?

□ known

□ solution

□ fact

□ mystery

8.29) What does 'facetious' mean in the sentence: 'His facetious remarks were not appreciated during the serious meeting'?

□ joking

□ thoughtful

□ sincere

□ serious

8.30) What does 'garrulous' mean in the sentence: 'The garrulous student was often scolded for talking during class'?

□ talkative

□ quiet

□ silent

□ reserved

8.31) What does 'hapless' mean in the sentence: 'The hapless tourist lost his wallet and missed his flight'?

□ careful

□ lucky

□ unfortunate

□ happy

8.32) What does 'idiosyncratic' mean in the sentence: 'Her idiosyncratic habits made her stand out from the crowd'?

□ typical

□ peculiar

□ common

□ boring

8.33) What does 'lugubrious' mean in the sentence: 'The lugubrious music set the tone for the sad movie'?

□ cheerful

□ upbeat

□ lively

□ mournful

8.34) What does 'mercurial' mean in the sentence: 'His mercurial temperament made him unpredictable'?

☐ stable

☐ consistent

☐ unpredictable

☐ calm

8.35) What does 'nefarious' mean in the sentence: 'The nefarious villain plotted to take over the world'?

☐ noble

☐ wicked

☐ heroic

☐ kind

8.36) What does 'ostentatious' mean in the sentence: 'Her ostentatious display of wealth was meant to impress'?

☐ showy

☐ humble

☐ modest

☐ plain

8.37) What does 'pugnacious' mean in the sentence: 'The pugnacious boxer was known for his aggressive style'?

□ gentle

□ aggressive

□ peaceful

□ calm

8.38) What does 'quintessential' mean in the sentence: 'She is the quintessential example of a successful entrepreneur'?

□ poor example

□ rare example

□ perfect example

□ difficult example

8.39) What does 'reticent' mean in the sentence: 'He was reticent to share his personal thoughts with the group'?

□ talkative

□ outgoing

□ friendly

□ reserved

8.40) What does 'supercilious' mean in the sentence: 'Her supercilious attitude made her unpopular among her peers'?

☐ modest

☐ arrogant

☐ humble

☐ kind

Topic 8 - Answers

Question Number	Answer	Explanation
8.1	run away	"Abscond" means to run away.
8.2	kind	"Benevolent" means kind.
8.3	harsh noise	"Cacophony" means harsh noise.
8.4	weaken	"Debilitate" means to weaken.
8.5	short-lived	"Ephemeral" means short-lived.
8.6	secretive	"Furtive" means secretive.
8.7	sociable	"Gregarious" means sociable.
8.8	sign	"Harbinger" means a sign.
8.9	place side by side	"Juxtapose" means to place side by side.
8.10	slow and relaxed	"Languid" means slow and relaxed.
8.11	sweet sounding	"Mellifluous" means sweet sounding.
8.12	unclear	"Nebulous" means unclear.
8.13	confuse	"Obfuscate" means to confuse.
8.14	harmful	"Pernicious" means harmful.
8.15	idealistic	"Quixotic" means idealistic.
8.16	stubbornly resistant	"Recalcitrant" means stubbornly resistant.
8.17	flatterer	"Sycophant" means flatterer.
8.18	perceptible	"Tangible" means perceptible.

8.19	everywhere	"Ubiquitous" means everywhere.
8.20	changes	"Vicissitude" means changes.
8.21	wrinkled	"Wizened" means wrinkled.
8.22	fear of strangers	"Xenophobia" means fear of strangers.
8.23	enthusiastic	"Zealous" means enthusiastic.
8.24	bitterness	"Acrimony" means bitterness.
8.25	trite	"Banal" means trite.
8.26	embarrassment	"Chagrin" means embarrassment.
8.27	different	"Disparate" means different.
8.28	mystery	"Enigma" means mystery.
8.29	joking	"Facetious" means joking.
8.30	talkative	"Garrulous" means talkative.
8.31	unfortunate	"Hapless" means unfortunate.
8.32	peculiar	"Idiosyncratic" means peculiar.
8.33	mournful	"Lugubrious" means mournful.
8.34	unpredictable	"Mercurial" means unpredictable.
8.35	wicked	"Nefarious" means wicked.
8.36	showy	"Ostentatious" means showy.
8.37	aggressive	"Pugnacious" means aggressive.
8.38	perfect example	"Quintessential" means perfect example.
8.39	reserved	"Reticent" means reserved.
8.40	arrogant	"Supercilious" means arrogant.

Ready for More?

The NWEA MAP testing is adaptive. This means that if your student found these questions too tricky or too easy, they may find it useful to practice grades below or above they grade they are in. This will expose students to new concepts and ideas, giving them a better chance at scoring higher in tests.

Alexander-Grace Education produces books covering Mathematics, Sciences, and English, to help your student maximize their potential in these areas.

For errata, please email
alexandergraceeducation@gmail.com

Made in United States
North Haven, CT
21 November 2024

60731973R00063